Help For Drug A

A Self-Help Book About Drug Addiction
Symptoms, Drug Abuse Intervention, Drug
Rehab, The 12 Step Program And Other
Treatments And Support For Drug Addiction
Recovery So You Can Heal Yourself From
Substance Abuse

By:

Yvette L. Bandry

Life can sometimes get very difficult and hard to take. Different people cope in different ways with the stress that life brings. Regrettably, drugs have become the most prominent coping mechanism that people use to deal with life's problems.

Drugs can be medical wonders if taken properly. They can cure our pains, aches and illnesses. They can also help us overcome some of our hang-ups and inhibitions. The problem begins when drugs are wrongly used.

The thing about drugs is that it makes you feel good about yourself and the world around you – even for just a little while – and then it traps you into a vicious cycle of craving. You start feeling that you can't live without the euphoria and ecstasy that drugs give you and that you just can't cope with life's problems without the drugs. That's the onset of abuse and addiction.

This guide is a self-help book for the drug addict and for those who have a love one with some form of substance addiction. You will get information on:

- The effects of methamphetamine, heroin, marijuana, cocaine, alcohol, nicotine, prescription drugs

- How to identify your drug problem
- How to identify the signs in others
- How addiction works
- Treatment options - rehab centers, safe detoxing, working the 12 steps, building your self-esteem
- Intervention, involving the family
- Calming the soul, staying sober

This book is a treatment guide so you can get the help you need to help yourself (or a love one) get clean and sober. We'll look at the signs of a problem and address the various drugs that are most likely to cause dependence. Then, with the help of experts, we'll give you some strategies that you can try to get you back on the road to a drug-free life.

Drug addiction is a powerful demon that can sneak up on you and take over your life. You can help yourself get out of it. Your journey to recovery starts with your choice!

Disclaimer And Terms Of Use Agreement

This information is not presented by a medical practitioner and is for educational and informational purposes only. The content is not intended to be a substitute for professional medical advice, diagnosis, or treatment. Always seek the advice of your physician or other qualified health care provider with any questions you may have regarding a medical condition. Never disregard professional medical advice or delay in seeking it because of something you have read or heard.

The author and publisher make no representation or warranties with respect to the accuracy, applicability, fitness, or completeness of the contents of this book. The information contained in this book is strictly for educational purposes. Therefore, if you wish to apply ideas contained in this book, you are taking full responsibility for your actions.

Every effort has been made to accurately represent this product and its potential. However, there is no guarantee that you will improve in any way using the techniques and ideas in these materials. Examples in these materials are not to be interpreted as a promise or guarantee of anything. Self-help and improvement potential is entirely dependent on the person using our product, ideas and techniques.

Many factors will be important in determining your actual results and no guarantees are made that you will achieve results similar to ours or anybody else's, in fact no guarantees are made that you will achieve any results from our ideas and techniques in our material.

The author and publisher disclaim any warranties (express or implied), merchantability, or fitness for any particular purpose. The author and publisher shall in no event be held liable to any party for any direct, indirect, punitive, special, incidental or other consequential damages arising directly or indirectly from any use of this material, which is provided "as is," and without warranties.

The author and publisher do not warrant the performance, effectiveness or applicability of any sites listed or linked to in this book. All links are for information purposes only and are not warranted for content, accuracy or any other implied or explicit purpose.

Table of Contents

Introduction

Life can be crazy. Life can be stressful. Life can be hard to take. These are all truths that are just simple facts. Because life can be difficult, people look for different ways to cope with the stress that life brings.

Regrettably, drugs have become the most prominent coping mechanism that people use to deal with life's problems. There are many reasons why people begin using drugs. They are looking for a way out – an escape – a way to forget life for just a little while.

Methamphetamine use has grown to alarming rates in the United States with over 25 percent of the population addicted to this drug. Twenty-three percent of high school seniors use marijuana on a regular basis. Forty-three percent of adults report having a problem with alcohol.

The statistics also reveal that drug use, including alcohol and cigarettes, is beginning earlier in life. Children are experimenting with drugs as young as 10 years old, and many middle schoolers have already had their first taste of alcohol by seventh grade.

What are even more disturbing are the health effects that drug use and abuse causes. Last year alone, there were over 20,000 alcohol-induced deaths not including car accidents, and deaths due to heroin overdoses have increased by two percent in just the course of one year.

Drug addiction doesn't discriminate either. Many famous celebrities have struggled with addiction as has the common man. You can be a regular housewife or the head of a company and find yourself struggling with drug dependence.

What can you do? The answer is – a lot. If you find yourself with a problem, the time to take action is now. You could check yourself into a rehabilitation facility, but you can also try some self-help steps first.

This book is intended for both the person who is addicted and for those who have a loved one with addiction. We'll look at the signs of a problem and address the various drugs that are most likely to cause dependence. Then, with the help of experts, we'll give you some strategies that you can try to get you back on the road to a drug-free life.

You can overcome your dependence on drugs. It won't be easy, but you can do it. But you have to start now. Don't be addicted anymore. Start your journey today!

Chapter 1 - Why People Use Drugs

The reasons people use drugs are varied. Essentially, though, drugs give us a desired effect producing a feeling of euphoria that makes us feel better – at least temporarily. There are hundreds of ways that drugs help people cope with life and each person has their own reason why they choose a certain drug.

Drugs can help calm you down, give you energy, overcome shyness, and avoid feelings of loneliness. They may you feel bolder and want to take risks you wouldn't normally take. They are used to perhaps fit into social situation and get into a "party" mood and even to celebrate happy occasions.

Medically, drugs are used to alleviate pain, help you to sleep, suppress anger, combat anxiety, and avoid depression. They can be used to cope with stress, stimulate your desire for sex, and lose weight.

Many people report that they began using drugs as a response to peer pressure. Those around them would use drugs, so to fit in, they began using as well.

The ways drugs affect us are countless—for everyone. So much so that often it seems that drugs can cure all our ills and help us overcome whatever bothers us. If that's all there were to it, we might consider each drug to be some kind of "wonder drug."

This is where the thought process gets a little skewed. People begin to crave the feeling of euphoria that they get when they use drugs and that's when it becomes a problem. It can be a vicious cycle. You feel you can't live without the feelings that drugs give you and that you just won't be able to cope with life without those drugs. That's what breeds addiction.

Let's look at various drugs of choice that people often use and what those specific drugs can do.

Chapter 2 - Methamphetamine

Methamphetamine is an addictive stimulant that is closely related to amphetamine, but has longer lasting and more toxic effects on the central nervous system. It has a high potential for abuse and addiction.

Methamphetamine use is on the rise around the country. It has reached epidemic proportions mainly because it is easy to make using common household items.

Meth is often referred to as speed, chalk, ice, crystal, and glass.

The drug increases wakefulness and physical activity and decreases appetite. Chronic, long-term use can lead to psychotic behavior, hallucinations, and stroke. People who use meth often don't sleep – sometimes for days on end. They lose weight quickly because the drug suppresses appetite.

Meth addicts often have lost some of their teeth, look gaunt, and will have sores on their body from nervous energy they are trying to get rid of.

National health statistics report that over 12 million Americans have tried methamphetamine with many of them quickly becoming addicted to the drug.

Methamphetamine is taken orally, intra-nasally (snorting the powder), by needle injection, or by smoking. Abusers may become addicted quickly, needing higher doses and more often.

Methamphetamine increases the release of very high levels of the neurotransmitter dopamine, which stimulates brain cells, enhancing mood and body movement. Chronic methamphetamine abuse significantly changes how the brain functions.

Animal research going back more than 30 years shows that high doses of methamphetamine damage neuron cell endings. Dopamine- and serotonin-containing neurons do not die after methamphetamine use, but their nerve endings ("terminals") are cut back, and re-growth appears to be limited.

Human brain imaging studies have shown alterations in the activity of the dopamine system. These alterations are associated with reduced motor speed and impaired verbal learning.

Recent studies in chronic methamphetamine abusers have also revealed severe structural and functional changes in areas of the brain associated with emotion and memory, which may account for many of the emotional and cognitive problems observed in chronic methamphetamine abusers.

Taking even small amounts of methamphetamine can result in increased respiration, rapid heart rate, irregular heartbeat, increased blood pressure, and hyperthermia. Other effects of methamphetamine abuse may include irritability, anxiety, insomnia, confusion, tremors, convulsions, and cardiovascular collapse and death.

As we've already indicated, long-term effects may include paranoia, aggressiveness, extreme anorexia, memory loss, visual and auditory hallucinations, delusions, and severe dental problems.

Also, transmission of HIV and hepatitis B and C can be a consequence of methamphetamine abuse. Among abusers who inject the drug, infection with HIV and other infectious diseases is spread mainly through the re-use of contaminated syringes, needles, and other injection equipment by more than one person.

The intoxicating effects of methamphetamine, however, whether it is injected or taken other ways, can alter judgment and inhibition and lead people to engage in unsafe behaviors. Methamphetamine abuse actually may worsen the progression of HIV and its consequences; studies with methamphetamine abusers who have HIV indicate that the HIV causes greater neuronal injury and cognitive impairment compared with HIV-positive people who do not use drugs.

Meth is a scary drug with horrible health implications.

Chapter 3 - Heroin

Heroin is an addictive drug that is processed from morphine and usually appears as a white or brown powder. Its street names include smack, H, ska, junk, and many others. Heroin use is on the rise and it has become a serious problem in America.

Heroin abuse is associated with serious health conditions, including fatal overdose, spontaneous abortion, collapsed veins, and, particularly in users who inject the drug, infectious diseases, including HIV/AIDS and hepatitis.

The short-term effects of heroin abuse appear soon after a single dose and disappear in a few hours. After an injection of heroin, the user reports feeling a surge of euphoria ("rush") accompanied by a warm flushing of the skin, a dry mouth, and heavy extremities.

Following this initial euphoria, the user goes "on the nod," an alternately wakeful and drowsy state. Mental functioning becomes clouded due to the depression of the central nervous system.

Long-term effects of heroin appear after repeated use for some period of time. Chronic users may develop collapsed veins, infection of the heart lining and valves, abscesses, cellulitis, and liver disease. Pulmonary complications, including various types of pneumonia, may result from the poor health condition of the abuser, as well as from heroin's depressing effects on respiration.

Heroin abuse during pregnancy and its many associated environmental factors (e.g., lack of prenatal care) have been associated with adverse consequences including low birth weight, an important risk factor for later developmental delay.

In addition to the effects of the drug itself, street heroin may have additives that do not readily dissolve and result in clogging the blood vessels that lead to the lungs, liver, kidneys, or brain. This can cause infection or even death of small patches of cells in vital organs.

The Drug Abuse Warning Network reports that eight percent of drug-related emergency department (ED) visits in the third and fourth quarters of 2003 involved heroin abuse. Unspecified opiates, which could include heroin, were involved in an additional 4 percent of drug-related visits.

With regular heroin use, tolerance develops. This means the abuser must use more to achieve the same intensity of effect. As higher doses are used over time, physical dependence and addiction develop. With physical dependence, the body has adapted to the presence of the drug and withdrawal symptoms may occur if use is reduced or stopped.

Withdrawal, which in regular abusers may occur as early as a few hours after the last administration, produces drug craving, restlessness, muscle and bone pain, insomnia, diarrhea and vomiting, cold flashes with goose bumps ("cold turkey"), kicking movements ("kicking the habit"), and other symptoms.

Major withdrawal symptoms peak between 48 and 72 hours after the last dose and subside after about a week. Sudden withdrawal by heavily dependent users who are in poor health is occasionally fatal, although heroin withdrawal is considered less dangerous than alcohol or barbiturate withdrawal.

Chapter 4 - Marijuana

There are a lot of people who are of the opinion that marijuana is not a harmful drug and that it should be as legal to buy and use as alcohol. Marijuana is the most commonly used illegal drug in the United States. Besides alcohol, marijuana is the most commonly used drug by young people.

Marijuana is a dry, shredded green/brown mix of flowers, stems, seeds, and leaves of the hemp plant Cannabis sativa, it usually is smoked as a cigarette (joint, nail), or in a pipe (bong). It also is smoked in blunts, which are cigars that have been emptied of tobacco and refilled with marijuana, often in combination with another drug. It might also be mixed in food or brewed as a tea.

As a more concentrated, resinous form it is called hashish and, as a sticky black liquid, hash oil. Marijuana smoke has a pungent and distinctive, usually sweet-and-sour odor. Some people think that the smoke smells like burning rope.

There are countless street terms for marijuana including pot, herb, weed, grass, widow, ganja, and hash, as well as terms derived from trademarked varieties of cannabis, such as Bubble Gum, Northern Lights, Fruity Juice, Afghani #1, and a number of Skunk varieties.

The main active chemical in marijuana is THC (delta-9-tetrahydrocannabinol). The membranes of certain nerve cells in the brain contain protein receptors that bind to THC. Once securely in place, THC kicks off a series of cellular reactions that ultimately lead to the high that users experience when they smoke marijuana.

Scientists have learned a great deal about how THC acts in the brain to produce its many effects. When someone smokes marijuana, THC rapidly passes from the lungs into the bloodstream, which carries the chemical to organs throughout the body, including the brain.

In the brain, THC connects to specific sites called cannabinoid receptors on nerve cells and influences the activity of those cells. Some brain areas have many cannabinoid receptors; others have few or none. Many cannabinoid receptors are found in the parts of the brain that influence pleasure, memory, thought, concentration, sensory and time perception, and coordinated movement[4].

The short-term effects of marijuana can include problems with memory and learning; distorted perception; difficulty in thinking and problem solving; loss of coordination; and increased heart rate. Research findings for long-term marijuana abuse indicate some changes in the brain similar to those seen after long-term abuse of other major drugs.

For example, cannabinoid (THC or synthetic forms of THC) withdrawal in chronically exposed animals leads to an increase in the activation of the stress-response system and changes in the activity of nerve cells containing dopamine. Dopamine neurons are involved in the regulation of motivation and reward, and are directly or indirectly affected by all drugs of abuse.

Marijuana can have an adverse effect on the heart. One study has indicated that an abuser's risk of heart attack more than quadruples in the first hour after smoking marijuana. The researchers suggest that such an effect might occur from marijuana's effects on blood pressure and heart rate and reduced oxygen-carrying capacity of blood.

A user's lungs are also affected. A study of 450 individuals found that people who smoke marijuana frequently but do not smoke tobacco have more health problems and miss more days of work than nonsmokers. Many of the extra sick days among the marijuana smokers in the study were for respiratory illnesses.

Even infrequent abuse can cause burning and stinging of the mouth and throat, often accompanied by a heavy cough. Someone who smokes marijuana regularly may have many of the same respiratory problems that tobacco smokers do, such as daily cough and phlegm production, more frequent acute chest illness, a heightened risk of lung infections, and a greater tendency to obstructed airways.

Smoking marijuana possibly increases the likelihood of developing cancer of the head or neck. A study comparing 173 cancer patients and 176 healthy individuals produced evidence that marijuana smoking doubled or tripled the risk of these cancers.

Marijuana abuse also has the potential to promote cancer of the lungs and other parts of the respiratory tract because it contains irritants and carcinogens. In fact, marijuana smoke contains 50 to 70 percent more carcinogenic hydrocarbons than does tobacco smoke.

It also induces high levels of an enzyme that converts certain hydrocarbons into their carcinogenic form—levels that may accelerate the changes that ultimately produce malignant cells.

Marijuana users usually inhale more deeply and hold their breath longer than tobacco smokers do, which increases the lungs' exposure to carcinogenic smoke. These facts suggest that, puff for puff, smoking marijuana may be more harmful to the lungs than smoking tobacco.

Some of marijuana's adverse health effects may occur because THC impairs the immune system's ability to fight disease. In laboratory experiments that exposed animal and human cells to THC or other marijuana ingredients, the normal disease-preventing reactions of many of the key types of immune cells were inhibited. In other studies, mice exposed to THC or related substances were more likely than unexposed mice to develop bacterial infections and tumors.

Research clearly demonstrates that marijuana has the potential to cause problems in daily life or make a person's existing problems worse. Depression, anxiety, and personality disturbances have been associated with chronic marijuana use.

Because marijuana compromises the ability to learn and remember information, the more a person uses marijuana the more he or she is likely to fall behind in accumulating intellectual, job, or social skills. Moreover, research has shown that marijuana's adverse impact on memory and learning can last for days or weeks after the acute effects of the drug wear off.

Students who smoke marijuana get lower grades and are less likely to graduate from high school, compared with their nonsmoking peers. A study of 129 college students found that, among those who smoked the drug at least 27 of the 30 days prior to being surveyed, critical skills related to attention, memory, and learning were significantly impaired, even after the students had not taken the drug for at least 24 hours.

These "heavy" marijuana abusers had more trouble sustaining and shifting their attention and in registering, organizing, and using information than did the study participants who had abused marijuana no more than 3 of the previous 30 days. As a result, someone who smokes marijuana every day may be functioning at a reduced intellectual level all of the time.

More recently, the same researchers showed that the ability of a group of long-term heavy marijuana abusers to recall words from a list remained impaired for a week after quitting, but returned to normal within 4 weeks. Thus, some cognitive abilities may be restored in individuals who quit smoking marijuana, even after long-term heavy use.

Workers who smoke marijuana are more likely than their coworkers to have problems on the job. Several studies associate workers' marijuana smoking with increased absences, tardiness, accidents, workers' compensation claims, and job turnover.

A study among postal workers found that employees who tested positive for marijuana on a pre-employment urine drug test had 55 percent more industrial accidents, 85 percent more injuries, and a 75-percent increase in absenteeism compared with those who tested negative for marijuana use.

In another study, heavy marijuana abusers reported that the drug impaired several important measures of life achievement including cognitive abilities, career status, social life, and physical and mental health.

Research has shown that some babies born to women who abused marijuana during their pregnancies display altered responses to visual stimuli, increased tremulousness, and a high-pitched cry, which may indicate neurological problems in development.

During the preschool years, marijuana-exposed children have been observed to perform tasks involving sustained attention and memory more poorly than non-exposed children do. In the school years, these children are more likely to exhibit deficits in problem-solving skills, memory, and the ability to remain attentive.

Long-term marijuana abuse can lead to addiction for some people. That is, they abuse the drug compulsively even though it interferes with family, school, work, and recreational activities.

Drug craving and withdrawal symptoms can make it hard for long-term marijuana smokers to stop abusing the drug. People trying to quit report irritability, sleeplessness, and anxiety. They also display increased aggression on psychological tests, peaking approximately one week after the last use of the drug.

Chapter 5 - Cocaine

Cocaine is a powerfully addictive drug that is snorted, sniffed, injected, or smoked. Crack is cocaine that has been processed from cocaine hydrochloride to a free base for smoking. Its street names include coke, snow, flake, blow, and many others.

Cocaine is a stimulant drug. The powdered, hydrochloride salt form of cocaine can be snorted or dissolved in water and injected. Crack is cocaine that has not been neutralized by an acid to make the hydrochloride salt. This form of cocaine comes in a rock crystal that can be heated and its vapors smoked. The term "crack" refers to the crackling sound heard when it is heated.

Regardless of how cocaine is used or how frequently, a user can experience acute cardiovascular or cerebrovascular emergencies, such as a heart attack or stroke, which could result in sudden death. Cocaine-related deaths are often a result of cardiac arrest or seizure followed by respiratory arrest.

Cocaine is a strong central nervous system stimulant that interferes with the re-absorption process of dopamine, a chemical messenger associated with pleasure and movement. The buildup of dopamine causes continuous stimulation of receiving neurons, which is associated with the euphoria commonly reported by cocaine abusers.

Physical effects of cocaine use include constricted blood vessels, dilated pupils, and increased temperature, heart rate, and blood pressure. The duration of cocaine's immediate euphoric effects, which include hyper-stimulation, reduced fatigue, and mental alertness, depends on the route of administration.

The faster the absorption of the drug, the more intense the high. On the other hand, the faster the absorption, the shorter the duration of action. The high from snorting might last 15 to 30 minutes, while that from smoking may last 5 to 10 minutes. Increased use can reduce the period of time a user feels high and increases the risk of addiction.

Some users of cocaine report feelings of restlessness, irritability, and anxiety. A tolerance to the "high" may develop—many addicts report that they seek but fail to achieve as much pleasure as they did from their first exposure.

Some users will increase their doses to intensify and prolong the euphoric effects. While tolerance to the high can occur, users can also become more sensitive to cocaine's anesthetic and convulsive effects without increasing the dose taken. This increased sensitivity may explain some deaths occurring after apparently low doses of cocaine.

Use of cocaine in a binge, during which the drug is taken repeatedly and at increasingly high doses, may lead to a state of increasing irritability, restlessness, and paranoia. This can result in a period of full-blown paranoid psychosis, in which the user loses touch with reality and experiences auditory hallucinations.

Other complications associated with cocaine use include disturbances in heart rhythm and heart attacks, chest pain and respiratory failure, strokes, seizures and headaches, and gastrointestinal complications such as abdominal pain and nausea. Because cocaine has a tendency to decrease appetite, many chronic users can become malnourished.

Different means of taking cocaine can produce different adverse effects. Regularly snorting cocaine, for example, can lead to loss of the sense of smell, nosebleeds, problems with swallowing, hoarseness, and a chronically runny nose.

Ingesting cocaine can cause severe bowel gangrene due to reduced blood flow. People who inject cocaine can experience severe allergic reactions and, as with all injecting drug users, are at increased risk for contracting HIV and other blood-borne diseases.

When people mix cocaine and alcohol, they are compounding the danger each drug poses and are unknowingly forming a complex chemical experiment within their bodies. NIDA-funded researchers have found that the human liver combines cocaine and alcohol and manufactures a third substance, cocaethylene that intensifies cocaine's euphoric effects, while potentially increasing the risk of sudden death.

Chapter 6 - Alcohol

Alcohol is one of the most commonly abused drug in the United States. For most people who drink, alcohol is a pleasant accompaniment to social activities. Moderate alcohol use—up to two drinks per day for men and one drink per day for women and older people—is not harmful for most adults. (A standard drink is one 12-ounce bottle or can of either beer or wine cooler, one 5-ounce glass of wine, or 1.5 ounces of 80-proof distilled spirits.)

Nonetheless, a large number of people get into serious trouble because of their drinking. Currently, nearly 14 million Americans—1 in every 13 adults— abuse alcohol or are alcoholic. Several million more adults engage in risky drinking that could lead to alcohol problems. These patterns include binge drinking and heavy drinking on a regular basis. In addition, 53 percent of men and women in the United States report that one or more of their close relatives have a drinking problem.

The consequences of alcohol misuse are serious—in many cases, life threatening. Heavy drinking can increase the risk for certain cancers, especially those of the liver, esophagus, throat, and larynx (voice box). Heavy drinking can also cause liver cirrhosis, immune system problems, brain damage, and harm to the fetus during pregnancy.

In addition, drinking increases the risk of death from automobile crashes as well as recreational and on-the-job injuries. Furthermore, both homicides and suicides are more likely to be committed by persons who have been drinking. In purely economic terms, alcohol-related problems cost society approximately $185 billion per year. In human terms, the costs cannot be calculated.

Alcoholism, also known as "alcohol dependence," is a disease that includes four symptoms:

- **Craving:** A strong need, or compulsion, to drink.

- **Loss of control:** The inability to limit one's drinking on any given occasion.

- **Physical dependence:** Withdrawal symptoms, such as nausea, sweating, shakiness, and anxiety, occur when alcohol use is stopped after a period of heavy drinking.

- **Tolerance:** The need to drink greater amounts of alcohol in order to "get high."

Although some people are able to recover from alcoholism without help, the majority of alcoholics need assistance. With treatment and support, many individuals are able to stop drinking and rebuild their lives.

Many people wonder why some individuals can use alcohol without problems but others cannot. One important reason has to do with genetics. Scientists have found that having an alcoholic family member makes it more likely that if you choose to drink you too may develop alcoholism.

Genes, however, are not the whole story. In fact, scientists now believe that certain factors in a person's environment influence whether a person with a genetic risk for alcoholism ever develops the disease. A person's risk for developing alcoholism can increase based on the person's environment, including where and how he or she lives; family, friends, and culture; peer pressure; and even how easy it is to get alcohol.

Alcohol abuse differs from alcoholism in that it does not include an extremely strong craving for alcohol, loss of control over drinking, or physical dependence. Alcohol abuse is defined as a pattern of drinking that result in one or more of the following situations within a 12-month period:

- Failure to fulfill major work, school, or home responsibilities

- Drinking in situations that are physically dangerous, such as while driving a car or operating machinery

- Having recurring alcohol-related legal problems, such as being arrested for driving under the influence of alcohol or for physically hurting someone while drunk

- Continued drinking despite having ongoing relationship problems that are caused or worsened by the drinking. Although alcohol abuse is basically different from alcoholism, many effects of alcohol abuse are also experienced by alcoholics.

Although alcoholism can be treated, a cure is not yet available. In other words, even if an alcoholic has been sober for a long time and has regained health, he or she remains susceptible to relapse and must continue to avoid all alcoholic beverages. "Cutting down" on drinking doesn't work; cutting out alcohol is necessary for a successful recovery.

However, even individuals who are determined to stay sober may suffer one or several "slips," or relapses, before achieving long-term sobriety. Relapses are very common and do not mean that a person has failed or cannot recover from alcoholism.

Keep in mind, too, that every day that a recovering alcoholic has stayed sober prior to a relapse is extremely valuable time, both to the individual and to his or her family. If a relapse occurs, it is very important to try to stop drinking once again and to get whatever additional support you need to abstain from drinking.

Chapter 7 - Nicotine

Through the use of cigarettes, cigars, and chewing tobacco, nicotine is one of the most heavily used addictive drugs in the United States. In 2004, 29.2 percent of the U.S. population 12 and older—70.3 million people—used tobacco at least once in the month prior to being interviewed.

This figure includes 3.6 million young people age 12 to 17. Young adults aged 18 to 25 reported the highest rate of current use of any tobacco products (44.6 percent) in 2004.

Findings for high school youth indicate that 25.9 percent of 8th-graders, 38.9 percent of 10th-graders, and 50.0 percent of 12th-graders had ever smoked cigarettes when asked in 2005. These figures were lower for all three grades from 2004 data, and for 8th-graders and 12th-graders, the decreases were statistically significant.

Statistics from the Centers for Disease Control and Prevention indicate that tobacco use remains the leading preventable cause of death in the United States, causing approximately 440,000 premature deaths each year and resulting in an annual cost of more than $75 billion in direct medical costs attributable to smoking.

Over the past four decades, cigarette smoking has caused an estimated 12 million deaths, including 4.1 million deaths from cancer, 5.5 million deaths from cardiovascular diseases, 2.1 million deaths from respiratory diseases, and 94,000 infant deaths related to mothers smoking during pregnancy.

Secondhand smoke, also known as environmental tobacco smoke, is a mixture of the smoke given off by the burning end of tobacco products (side stream smoke) and the mainstream smoke exhaled by smokers. It is a complex mixture containing many chemicals (including formaldehyde, cyanide, carbon monoxide, ammonia, and nicotine), many of which are known carcinogens.

Nonsmokers exposed to secondhand smoke at home or work increase their risk of developing heart disease by 25 to 30 percent and lung cancer by 20 to 30 percent.

In addition, secondhand smoke causes respiratory problems in nonsmokers such as coughing, phlegm, and reduced lung function. Children exposed to secondhand smoke are at an increased risk for sudden infant death syndrome, acute respiratory infections, ear problems, and more severe asthma.

Since 1964, 28 Surgeon General's reports on smoking and health have concluded that tobacco use is the single most avoidable cause of disease, disability, and death in the United States. In 1988, the Surgeon General concluded that cigarettes and other forms of tobacco, such as cigars, pipe tobacco, and chewing tobacco, are addictive and that nicotine is the drug in tobacco that causes addiction.

Nicotine provides an almost immediate "kick" because it causes a discharge of epinephrine from the adrenal cortex. This stimulates the central nervous system and endocrine glands, which causes a sudden release of glucose. Stimulation is then followed by depression and fatigue, leading the user to seek more nicotine.

Nicotine is absorbed readily from tobacco smoke in the lungs, and it does not matter whether the tobacco smoke is from cigarettes, cigars, or pipes. Nicotine also is absorbed readily when tobacco is chewed. With regular use of tobacco, levels of nicotine accumulate in the body during the day and persist overnight. Thus, daily smokers or chewers are exposed to the effects of nicotine for 24 hours each day. Adolescents who chew tobacco are more likely than nonusers to eventually become cigarette smokers.

Addiction to nicotine results in withdrawal symptoms when a person tries to stop smoking. For example, a study found that when chronic smokers were deprived of cigarettes for 24 hours, they had increased anger, hostility, and aggression, and loss of social cooperation. Persons suffering from withdrawal also take longer to regain emotional equilibrium following stress. During periods of abstinence and/or craving, smokers have shown impairment across a wide range of psychomotor and cognitive functions, such as language comprehension.

Women who smoke generally have earlier menopause. Pregnant women who smoke cigarettes run an increased risk of having stillborn or premature infants or infants with low birth weight. Children of women who smoked while pregnant have an increased risk for developing conduct disorders. National studies of mothers and daughters have also found that maternal smoking during pregnancy increased the probability that female children would smoke and would persist in smoking.

In addition to nicotine, cigarette smoke is primarily composed of a dozen gases (mainly carbon monoxide) and tar. The tar in a cigarette, which varies from about 15 mg for a regular cigarette to 7 mg in a low-tar cigarette, exposes the user to an increased risk of lung cancer, emphysema, and bronchial disorders.

The carbon monoxide in tobacco smoke increases the chance of cardiovascular diseases. The Environmental Protection Agency has concluded that secondhand smoke causes lung cancer in adults and greatly increases the risk of respiratory illnesses in children and sudden infant death.

Research has shown that nicotine, like cocaine, heroin, and marijuana, increases the level of the neurotransmitter dopamine, which affects the brain pathways that control reward and pleasure. Scientists have pinpointed a particular molecule [the beta 2 (b2)] subunit of the nicotine cholinergic receptor as a critical component in nicotine addiction.

Mice that lack this subunit fail to self-administer nicotine, implying that without the b2 subunit, the mice do not experience the positive reinforcing properties of nicotine. This finding identifies a potential site for targeting the development of nicotine addiction medications.

Other research found that individuals have greater resistance to nicotine addiction if they have a genetic variant that decreases the function of the enzyme CYP2A6. The decrease in CYP2A6 slows the breakdown of nicotine and protects individuals against nicotine addiction.

Understanding the role of this enzyme in nicotine addiction gives a new target for developing more effective medications to help people stop smoking. Medications might be developed that can inhibit the function of CYP2A6, thus providing a new approach to preventing and treating nicotine addiction.

Another study found dramatic changes in the brain's pleasure circuits during withdrawal from chronic tobacco use. These changes are comparable in magnitude and duration to similar changes observed during withdrawal from other abused drugs such as cocaine, opiates, amphetamines, and alcohol.

Scientists found significant decreases in the sensitivity of the brains of laboratory rats to pleasurable stimulation after nicotine administration was abruptly stopped. These changes lasted several days and may correspond to the anxiety and depression experienced by humans for several days after quitting smoking "cold turkey."

The results of this research may help in the development of better treatments for the withdrawal symptoms that may interfere with individuals' attempts to quit.

Chapter 8 - Prescription Drugs

Prescription medications such as pain relievers, tranquilizers, stimulants, and sedatives are very useful treatment tools, but sometimes people do not take them as directed and may become addicted. Pain relievers make surgery possible, and enable many individuals with chronic pain to lead productive lives.

Most people who take prescription medications use them responsibly. However, the inappropriate or non-medical use of prescription medications is a serious public health concern. Non-medical use of prescription medications like opioids, central nervous system (CNS) depressants, and stimulants can lead to addiction, characterized by compulsive drug seeking and use.

Patients, healthcare professionals, and pharmacists all have roles in preventing misuse and addiction to prescription medications. For example, when a doctor prescribes a pain relief medication, CNS depressant, or stimulant, the patient should follow the directions for use carefully, learn what effects the medication could have, and determine any potential interactions with other medications.

The patient should read all information provided by the pharmacist. Physicians and other healthcare providers should screen for any type of substance abuse during routine history-taking, with questions about which prescriptions and over-the-counter (OTC) medicines the patient is taking and why.

Providers should note any rapid increases in the amount of a medication needed or frequent requests for refills before the quantity prescribed should have been used, as these may be indicators of abuse.

While many prescription medications can be abused or misused, these three classes are most commonly abused:

- **Opioids** - often prescribed to treat pain.

- **CNS Depressants** - used to treat anxiety and sleep disorders.

- **Stimulants** - prescribed to treat narcolepsy and attention deficit/hyperactivity disorder.

Opioids

Opioids are commonly prescribed because of their effective analgesic, or pain relieving, properties. Studies have shown that properly managed medical use of opioid analgesic compounds is safe and rarely causes addiction. Taken exactly as prescribed, opioids can be used to manage pain effectively.

Among the compounds that fall within this class — sometimes referred to as narcotics — are morphine, codeine, and related medications. Morphine is often used before or after surgery to alleviate severe pain. Codeine is used for milder pain.

Other examples of opioids that can be prescribed to alleviate pain include oxycodone (OxyContin — an oral, controlled release form of the drug); propoxyphene (Darvon); hydrocodone (Vicodin); hydromorphone (Dilaudid); and meperidine (Demerol), which is used less often because of its side effects.

In addition to their effective pain relieving properties, some of these medications can be used to relieve severe diarrhea (Lomotil, for example, which is diphenoxylate) or severe coughs (codeine).

Opioids act by attaching to specific proteins called opioid receptors, which are found in the brain, spinal cord, and gastrointestinal tract. When these compounds attach to certain opioid receptors in the brain and spinal cord, they can effectively change the way a person experiences pain.

In addition, opioid medications can affect regions of the brain that mediate what we perceive as pleasure, resulting in the initial euphoria that many opioids produce. They can also produce drowsiness, cause constipation, and, depending upon the amount taken, depress breathing. Taking a large single dose could cause severe respiratory depression or death.

Opioids may interact with other medications and are only safe to use with other medications under a physician's supervision. Typically, they should not be used with substances such as alcohol, antihistamines, barbiturates, or benzodiazepines. Since these substances slow breathing, their combined effects could lead to life-threatening respiratory depression.

Long-term use also can lead to physical dependence—the body adapts to the presence of the substance and withdrawal symptoms occur if use is reduced abruptly. This can also include tolerance, which means that higher doses of a medication must be taken to obtain the same initial effects.

Note that physical dependence is not the same as addiction—physical dependence can occur even with appropriate long-term use of opioid and other medications. Addiction, as noted earlier, is defined as compulsive, often uncontrollable drug use in spite of negative consequences.

Individuals taking prescribed opioid medications should not only be given these medications under appropriate medical supervision, but also should be medically supervised when stopping use in order to reduce or avoid withdrawal symptoms.

Symptoms of withdrawal can include restlessness, muscle and bone pain, insomnia, diarrhea, vomiting, cold flashes with goose bumps ("cold turkey"), and involuntary leg movements.

Individuals who become addicted to prescription medications can be treated. Options for effectively treating addiction to prescription opioids are drawn from research on treating heroin addiction. Some pharmacological examples of available treatments follow:

- Methadone, a synthetic opioid that blocks the effects of heroin and other opioids, eliminates withdrawal symptoms and relieves craving. It has been used for over 30 years to successfully treat people addicted to opioids.

- Buprenorphine, another synthetic opioid, is a recent addition to the arsenal of medications for treating addiction to heroin and other opiates.

- Naltrexone is a long-acting opioid blocker often used with highly motivated individuals in treatment programs promoting complete abstinence. Naltrexone also is used to prevent relapse.

- Naloxone counteracts the effects of opioids and is used to treat overdoses.

Central Nervous System (CNS) Depressants

CNS depressants slow normal brain function. In higher doses, some CNS depressants can become general anesthetics. Tranquilizers and sedatives are examples of CNS depressants.

CNS depressants can be divided into two groups, based on their chemistry and pharmacology:

- Barbiturates, such as mephobarbital (Mebaral) and pentobarbitalsodium (Nembutal), which are used to treat anxiety, tension, and sleep disorders.

- Benzodiazepines, such as diazepam (Valium), chlordiazepoxide HCl (Librium), and alprazolam (Xanax), which can be prescribed to treat anxiety, acute stress reactions, and panic attacks.

Benzodiazepines that have a more sedating effect, such as estazolam (ProSom), can be prescribed for short-term treatment of sleep disorders.

There are many CNS depressants, and most act on the brain similarly—they affect the neurotransmitter gamma-aminobutyric acid (GABA). Neurotransmitters are brain chemicals that facilitate communication between brain cells. GABA works by decreasing brain activity.

Although different classes of CNS depressants work in unique ways, ultimately it is their ability to increase GABA activity that produces a drowsy or calming effect. Despite these beneficial effects for people suffering from anxiety or sleep disorders, barbiturates and benzodiazepines can be addictive and should be used only as prescribed.

CNS depressants should not be combined with any medication or substance that causes drowsiness, including prescription pain medicines, certain OTC cold and allergy medications, or alcohol. If combined, they can slow breathing, or slow both the heart and respiration, which can be fatal.

Discontinuing prolonged use of high doses of CNS depressants can lead to withdrawal. Because they work by slowing the brain's activity, a potential consequence of abuse is that when one stops taking a CNS depressant, the brain's activity can rebound to the point that seizures can occur.

Someone thinking about ending their use of a CNS depressant, or who has stopped and is suffering withdrawal, should speak with a physician and seek medical treatment.

In addition to medical supervision, counseling in an in-patient or out-patient setting can help people who are overcoming addiction to CNS depressants. For example, cognitive-behavioral therapy has been used successfully to help individuals in treatment for abuse of benzodiazepines.

This type of therapy focuses on modifying a patient's thinking, expectations, and behaviors while simultaneously increasing their skills for coping with various life stressors.

Often the abuse of CNS depressants occurs in conjunction with the abuse of another substance or drug, such as alcohol or cocaine. In these cases of poly-drug abuse, the treatment approach should address the multiple addictions.

Stimulants

Stimulants increase alertness, attention, and energy, which are accompanied by increases in blood pressure, heart rate, and respiration.

Historically, stimulants were used to treat asthma and other respiratory problems, obesity, neurological disorders, and a variety of other ailments. As their potential for abuse and addiction became apparent, the use of stimulants began to wane.

Now, stimulants are prescribed for treating only a few health conditions, including narcolepsy, attention-deficit hyperactivity disorder (ADHD), and depression that has not responded to other treatments. Stimulants may also be used for short-term treatment of obesity and for patients with asthma.

Stimulants such as dextroamphetamine (Dexedrine) and methylphenidate (Ritalin) have chemical structures that are similar to key brain neurotransmitters called monoamines, which include norepinephrine and dopamine.

Stimulants increase the levels of these chemicals in the brain and body. This, in turn, increases blood pressure and heart rate, constricts blood vessels, increases blood glucose, and opens up the pathways of the respiratory system. In addition, the increase in dopamine is associated with a sense of euphoria that can accompany the use of stimulants.

Research indicates that people with ADHD do not become addicted to stimulant medications, such as Ritalin, when taken in the form and dosage prescribed. However, when misused, stimulants can be addictive.

The consequences of stimulant abuse can be extremely dangerous. Taking high doses of a stimulant can result in an irregular heartbeat, dangerously high body temperatures, and/or the potential for cardiovascular failure or seizures. Taking high doses of some stimulants repeatedly over a short period of time can lead to hostility or feelings of paranoia in some individuals.

Stimulants should not be mixed with antidepressants or OTC cold medicines containing decongestants. Antidepressants may enhance the effects of a stimulant, and stimulants in combination with decongestants may cause blood pressure to become dangerously high or lead to irregular heart rhythms.

Treatment of addiction to prescription stimulants, such as methylphenidate and amphetamines, is based on behavioral therapies proven effective for treating cocaine or methamphetamine addiction. At this time, there are no proven medications for the treatment of stimulant addiction. Antidepressants, however, may be used to manage the symptoms of depression that can accompany early abstinence from stimulants.

Depending on the patient's situation, the first step in treating prescription stimulant addiction may be to slowly decrease the drug's dose and attempt to treat withdrawal symptoms. This process of detoxification could then be followed with one of many behavioral therapies.

Contingency management, for example, improves treatment outcomes by enabling patients to earn vouchers for drug-free urine tests; the vouchers can be exchanged for items that promote healthy living. Cognitive-behavioral therapies, which teach patients skills to recognize risky situations, avoid drug use, and cope more effectively with problems, are proving beneficial. Recovery support groups may also be effective in conjunction with a behavioral therapy.

Now that you have an overview of various drugs that can become addictive, let's see if you or a loved one might have a problem.

Chapter 9 - Identifying Your Drug Problem

When you use drugs, they can quickly become a problem. Addiction can happen before you know it. You need to really take a look at your drug use and be honest with yourself when evaluating whether or not that drug use has become a problem.

Start by asking yourself one simple question: "Do you sometimes think you have a drug problem?" If the answer is yes, you probably do have an issue with addiction. Why?

Most of the time, drug abusers deny they have a problem, or they hide from it by making excuses. It's a natural reaction to defend yourself and your behaviors. But your defenses break down once in a while. So if you *sometimes* think you have a problem, you almost certainly do.

Think about how you feel the morning after heavy using. Your body aches, your head is cloudy, you feel guilty for over-using and promise yourself you'll stop. You decide that you won't be using drugs that day. You feel beaten and broken and want to do something about it. Your defenses are down and you are vulnerable to your own rational thoughts.

As the day goes on, though, your defenses start coming back up again and you begin excusing yourself for the previous day's binge. You start to make excuses for your over-indulgence. You tell yourself you were having a bad day, you didn't eat enough, you were really stressed out, or some other excuse.

You decide to let yourself use "just a little". After all, you were having a bad day yesterday. Today won't be the same. And the cycle continues.

You may go through this hundreds of time before you recognize that there's a pattern going on. Almost all drug abusers go through this cycle. When you decide to really face the possibility that you have a problem, how do you identify it? The answer is really quite simple.

You have a problem when you use too much, too often, and the use is out of control. But you have to be your own judge and be honest with yourself. Pay attention to your feelings. You may want to write down how you feel about your drug use. Sometimes seeing the words can help you face the problem and start helping yourself.

Let's take a look at a few questions that can help you identify if you have a drug problem. Answer the following questions honestly.

1) Have you ever felt you should cut down on your drug use?

2) Do you ever use drugs when you're alone?

3) Have you ever used more of a drug than you intended in a given period of time?

4) Have you ever used drugs for a longer period of time than you originally intended?

5) Have you ever used more than one drug at a time?

6) Concerning your use of drugs, has anyone ever told you that you use too much?

7) Have you ever taken one drug to overcome the effects of another?

8) Have you ever thought that your life might be better if you didn't take drugs?

9) Have you ever felt angry at yourself or guilty because of your drug use?

10) Do you regularly use a drug at certain times of the day or on certain occasions, for example, when you go to bed, when you wake up, before or after a meal, or before or after sex?

11) Have you ever lied about your drug use to family members or friends?

12) Have you ever lied to a doctor or faked symptoms to get prescription drugs?

13) Have you ever stolen drugs?

14) Have you ever stolen money or material goods that you could sell to obtain drugs?

15) Have you ever done things to obtain drugs that you later regretted?

16) Has your drug use ever caused problems for you with school or with work?

17) Have you noticed that you need to use more and more of a drug to get you high?

18) Do you experience withdrawal symptoms when you go without drugs for a few days?

19) Do you panic when your drug supply gets low?

20) Have you ever done something when you were high that you felt guilty about later?

21) Have you ever gotten into fights when high on drugs?

22) Have you ever been arrested for any drug-related activity (including possession)?

23) Have you ever been diagnosed with a medical problem related to your drug use?

24) Have you ever overdosed on a drug?

25) Have you ever attended a treatment program specifically related to drug use?

26) Have you associated with people with whom you normally wouldn't just so you could have access to drugs?

27) Have you stopped associating with any of your friends because they don't use drugs as much as you?

If you answered Yes to any two of these questions, this is a sign that you have a problem with drugs. If you answered Yes to any three, the chances are that you do have a problem with drugs. If you answered Yes to four or more, you definitely have a problem with drugs.

But this test is just a tool. You have become addicted to drugs when you start needing more of the drug to get the same effects, and you start to feel like you can't get along without that drug. You may try to quit, but the withdrawal symptoms are just too much to take so you continue using.

Another good way to identify a drug addiction problem is to write things down. Again, you need to be brutally honest with yourself when you answer the following questions. Take your time and list everything you can think of. The purpose of this exercise is to realize what your addiction has done to your life.

1) History: Go back to the start of your alcohol or drug addiction history. List each drug, and alcohol individually and trace the pattern of your life. What age did you start? When did you start increasing either the quantity or

frequency of each drug? This will show you if you have increased tolerance and if you have become dependent on which drugs.

Something to be noted is that if you have been only addicted to marijuana, if you decide to quit the marijuana and start alcohol, there is a high probability that you will again become addicted with time. If you have a family history of alcoholism or drug addiction you may be more susceptible to dependency. Part of this is genetic and also a learned model.

2) <u>Health</u>: Look at your physical health. List effects or any accidents, which may have been due to alcohol or drug use.

3) <u>Concerned Persons</u>: Think of comments others have made and the effect you have made on them because of your alcohol or drug addiction. Did you miss birthdays? Did you break promises? List each person personally and what effects you remember.

4) <u>Irrational, or Dangerous Behavior</u>: List times you took careless actions that put yourself or others in danger. List things you would not do

if not using alcohol or drugs.

5) <u>Sex</u>: Look at your sex life. Did your addiction to drugs or alcohol allow you to have sex without knowing someone? Did you take health risks such as lack of birth control or unprotected sex? Did the use of alcohol or drugs put you in danger of STD's and Aids?

6) <u>Work</u>: List examples of days missed, late, quitting or being fired from work. Did you get demoted, laid off or miss promotions or pay raises due to drug or alcohol use?

7) <u>Social Life and Friends</u>: How have your social activities and friends changed while using alcohol or drugs. Did you lose or drift away from drinkers or drug users? Did you become a part of a drug culture? Did you miss your partner's or children's activities when they wanted you to participate?

8) <u>Money</u>: Write down all legal costs, treatment expenses, loss of work pay, and how much you spent weekly on your alcohol or drug addiction. Add the years up to determine the loss. You may find you could own a house or

have a large savings with the money spent on alcohol and drugs.

9) Preoccupation: Did you start looking forward to or leaving work early to get alcohol or drugs? Did you use alcohol or drugs on the way to, or during work? Did you hide your drugs so nobody could use or throw them away?

10) Control: Did you make promises to cut down on either drugs or alcohol and not be able to? Did you quit after a DUI and then begin again?

11) Emotions and Feelings: What did alcohol and drug use do to your feelings? List the way they affected fear, anger, love, guilt, depression, loneliness and hurt. What is the difference between when you are using alcohol or drugs and sober?

12) Spiritual and Character: How are you different from what you desired or planned your life to be at this age. Are you divorced, giving up on God and full of selfishness for only the addiction and you? What are your spiritual beliefs? Write them down, and if you are able,

ask God to help remove your alcohol or drug addiction for things that build yourself and others up.

13)

A good ending to the alcohol and drug recovery plan is to write a Dear John letter to the alcohol or drug addiction itself. List what they did for your life including the damage and why you need to say good bye.

If you have a loved one you suspect is struggling with a drug problem, how do you recognize that problem?

Chapter 10 - Signs In Others

You can recognize signs of drug abuse in those around you by paying attention to their behavior. Read over the test above and see if you can identify any of the symptoms of a drug problem. Alienation from others, severe changes in behavior, increased defensives are all signs that a user has a problem.

Drug addicts will give up previously enjoyable activities that they would participate in. Their lives will become consumed with getting drugs and using drugs. Their physical appearance will change drastically. They will start missing work or school and the quality of their work will suffer.

To help you identify what type of drug your loved one might be using, here are some common outward signs of specific drugs.

Marijuana

- Rapid, loud talking and bursts of laughter in early stages of intoxication

- Sleepy or stuporous in the later stages

- Forgetfulness in conversation

- Inflammation in whites of eyes; pupils unlikely to be dilated

- Odor similar to burnt rope on clothing or breath

- Tendency to drive slowly — below speed limit

- Distorted sense of time passage — tendency to overestimate time intervals

- Use or possession of paraphernalia including roach clip, packs of rolling papers, pipes or bongs

Stimulants (Cocaine, Amphetamines, Methamphetamines)

- Dilated pupils (when large amounts are taken)

- Dry mouth and nose, bad breath, frequent lip licking

- Excessive activity, difficulty sitting still, lack of interest in food or sleep

- Irritable, argumentative, nervous

- Talkative, but conversation often lacks continuity; changes subjects rapidly

- Runny nose, cold or chronic sinus/nasal problems, nose bleeds

- Use or possession of paraphernalia including small spoons, razor blades, mirror, little bottles of white powder and plastic, glass or metal straws

Depressants (Barbiturates, Benzodiazapines)

- Symptoms of alcohol intoxication with no alcohol odor on breath (remember that depressants are frequently used with alcohol)

- Lack of facial expression or animation

- Flat affect

- Flaccid appearance

- Slurred speech

Narcotics (Heroin, Codeine, Morphine, Vicodin)

- Lethargy, drowsiness

- Constricted pupils fail to respond to light

- Redness and raw nostrils from inhaling heroin in power form

- Scars (tracks) on inner arms or other parts of body, from needle injections

- Use or possession of paraphernalia, including syringes, bent spoons, bottle caps, eye droppers, rubber tubing, cotton and needles

- Slurred speech

Hallucinogens (LSD, mescaline)

- Extremely dilated pupils

- Warm skin, excessive perspiration and body odor

- Distorted sense of sight, hearing, touch; distorted image of self and time perception

- Mood and behavior changes, the extent depending on emotional state of the user and environmental conditions

- Unpredictable flashback episodes even long after withdrawal (although these are rare)

Dissociative Anesthetics (PCP)

- Unpredictable behavior; mood may swing from passiveness to violence for no apparent reason

- Symptoms of intoxication

- Disorientation; agitation and violence if exposed to excessive sensory stimulation

- Fear, terror

- Rigid muscles

- Strange gait

- Deadened sensory perception (may experience severe injuries while appearing not to notice)

- Pupils may appear dilated

- Mask like facial appearance

- Floating pupils, appear to follow a moving object

- Comatose (unresponsive) if large amount consumed; eyes may be open or closed

Inhalants (Glue, Vapor producing solvents, Propellants)

- Substance odor on breath and clothes

- Runny nose

- Watering eyes

- Drowsiness or unconsciousness

- Poor muscle control

- Prefers group activity to being alone

- Presence of bags or rags containing dry plastic cement or other solvent at home, in locker at school or at work

- Discarded whipped cream, spray paint or similar chargers (users of nitrous oxide)

- Small bottles labeled "incense" (users of butyl nitrite)

So you think you or someone you love could possibly be addicted to drugs. You may wonder, "How in the world did it get this bad?"

Chapter 11 - How Addiction Works

Medical research shows two major causes of physical addiction. First, your cells adapt to the drug and, second, your metabolism becomes more efficient.

To your cells, the drugs you're using become a way of life. Every time you use a drug, your blood carries it to every cell in your body. Your cells adjust. They grow to expect these doses on schedule.

Your cells learn to cope with various drugs by defending themselves against the drugs' toxic effects. Cell walls harden to retain stability and reduce toxic damage. But as your cells get tough against drugs, gradually more and more can be consumed. Your tolerance increases.

In the long run, however, cell walls break down. At this point, your cells not only lose their ability to keep toxins out but also become unable to retain essential nutrients. Many of them stop functioning altogether or start functioning abnormally. That's when your organs (heart, brain, liver, or lungs), which are nothing more than whole systems of cells, begin to fail.

The problem with metabolism is that it is intimately connected to diet. Your body metabolizes food (breaks it down into its constituent parts) to get vital nutrients to all the cells. To serve this purpose, your body can metabolize many different foods and can learn how to gain nutrients from almost any kind of food you give it.

Metabolism also helps to rid the body of unwanted toxins. The liver is the key organ in this process. The liver "sees" drugs as unwanted toxins and begins producing enzymes that will help eliminate them from the body. It produces a different combination of enzymes for each drug. Moreover, the liver becomes extremely efficient at producing these enzymes. The more it "sees" a particular drug, the more efficiently it produces the enzymes that inactivate that drug.

Thus, a drug that you use often will get eliminated from the body with greater and greater efficiency. It's as if the liver begins to "expect" that drug and has enzymes ready and waiting. This is a key reason that tolerance increases, that is, why it takes greater and greater doses of a drug to get the same original effects.

Yet your personal metabolism works differently from anyone else's. Studies show that each individual has a unique biochemical makeup and that individuals differ greatly from one another in the way they metabolize different foods, drugs, or toxins.

To give you an idea how much possible variation there is, researchers have presently identified over 3,000 metabolic substances (called "metabolites") and over 1,100 enzymes. Each individual has different proportions of all 4,100 of these bio-chemicals. Of the enzymes, only about 30 are responsible for metabolizing all drugs.

Also, the mixture of bio-chemicals varies for each kind of food you ingest. For example, your body uses different bio-chemicals to metabolize the different classes of foods: meats, grains, vegetables, beans, fruits, and nuts. As you might have guessed, you need a whole different biochemical preparedness to handle drugs, alcohol, sugars, chemical additives, and toxins.

However, your body adjusts to whatever diet you give it, and the most frequent foods in your diet come to be expected. Biochemical pathways become established the more they are used. Thus, if your body doesn't get an expected food, you actually begin to crave it.

In fact, your body becomes addicted to the foods you give it the most. Your metabolism so completely adjusts to your regular diet that any change from this diet becomes increasingly difficult. Ask anyone who has attempted a major shift in diet.

For example, if you eat meat regularly, your metabolism will take a long time to adjust to a vegetarian diet. Although the same nutrients are available, your body doesn't have the biochemical preparedness. The ability is there. Your body can metabolize vegetarian meals. No problem. But to gain the same efficiency with a new diet can take from one to seven years.

The important thing to remember is this: Metabolism depends on diet. For our purposes, "diet" includes not only the nutritious foods but also the non-nutritious foods, such as sugar and alcohol, as well as other substances, such as chemical additives in foods, environmental toxins, and drugs.

You can change your metabolism if you change your diet. Although it will take a long time to change your metabolism significantly, you'll feel incredible improvements after just a few months. You'll discover the kinds of changes you need to make in a later chapter.

We become addicted to drugs partly as a way to avoid life's misery. In our minds at least, we become unwilling to suffer.

Real life is loaded with suffering. We not only experience myriad physical pains but also must cope with psychological pain. Many events make us ache inside. Things happen that cause us to feel sad, miserable, angry, nervous, tense, disgusted, confused, weakened, tortured, cheated, abused, frightened, or upset.

But we can avoid these feelings—at least for the moment—-by using drugs. We can do drugs and almost instantly feel "high." We can forget about life for a while. We can experience pleasure, excitement, power, courage, thrills, joy, enchantment, and a sense of connection with other people and the world around us.

Of course, in the long run drugs become less and less effective at bringing these benefits. Over time, the drugs themselves start causing suffering. Soon, we find we're using drugs to relieve the misery that drugs themselves have caused. This is known as the "vicious cycle of addiction."

It goes something like this: Life doesn't feel too good. Bang! Try this drug or that drug, and things feel better. Come down off the drug, and things feel worse, just a little worse than they did before you took the drug in the first place. No matter. Bang! Use the drug and feel good again.

Gradually, your biochemistry changes. Your brain learns that it doesn't have to keep producing the chemicals that make you feel good. These chemicals keep appearing without the brain having to do any work. That's why each time you try to get off the drugs, you feel a little worse than the time before. It becomes harder and harder for you to get off the drugs because you feel so bad whenever you try to stop.

And it all started with suffering, with your inability to accept suffering as an intimate part of life. You can break a drug habit anywhere along the way, or never start with drugs at all, simply by accepting life's suffering and facing the suffering head-on.

This doesn't mean that you will live a sad, miserable, and tormented life. There are plenty of ways you can face your suffering and then cope with it. In fact, once you learn these ways and begin using some of them, you'll feel as if your spirit has been renewed. Of course, it's your choice.

If you choose drugs to cope with life's suffering, you choose a buy-now-pay-later method. It works in the moment, but it just postpones the suffering. And by postponing it, it builds up, so that when you finally do face it, the suffering is immense.

The detoxification from drugs might take a week or two, but the long-term withdrawal, the period of time when your biochemistry (and thus your physical and mental health) returns to normal, can take years. Luckily, during this time, you gradually feel a little bit better, day by day.

What can you do to get help? You have many options. First, let's consider an in-patient rehabilitation facility.

Chapter 12 - Rehab Centers

Short-term residential programs were originally developed to treat alcoholism, but expanded to include drug addiction with the rise of cocaine use in the mid-1980s. Since then, they have been applied to a variety of drug addictions. They are set up to be intense, but relatively brief programs of between 3 and 6 months.

Most are based on the Minnesota Model, a method of drug addiction treatment that grew out of the success of the Alcoholics Anonymous, or 12-step model, of recovery. The elements of the Minnesota Model typically include:

- Thorough assessment of all aspects of a client: physical, emotional, mental, behavioral

- A personalized treatment plan for each participant

- Attendance of 12-step meetings and application of the 12-step philosophy

- Self-reflection with an emphasis on greater acceptance of personal responsibility, changing negative beliefs about self and others, and learning new coping skills

- Group and individual therapy (80-90% done in groups)

- Family support, education, and involvement

- Extensive outpatient follow up and support

The Minnesota Model is conducted by a multidisciplinary team of professionals - chemical dependency counselors, psychologists, psychiatrists, nurses, etc. The purpose of the model is to enable addicted individuals to achieve a significant transformation in their basic thinking, feeling and acting in relation to themselves and others. The resulting life change is identified as basically spiritual, though non-religious, in nature and is associated with the positive influence of group affiliation.

Drug rehab centers will address your problems specifically. There's a reason why you began using drugs and why you became addicted. These issues will be addressed and you will be learning new ways to cope with stressors besides using drugs.

Many rehab facilities are located in peaceful places with lush, green lawns, plenty of room to move about, and allow for concentration on becoming healthy outside the stress and anxiety of the city.

Some centers provide activities like boating, fishing, and sports for their patients. By offering these types of activities on the drug rehab center's property, patients can find the comfort and support they need to improve and change their lives by staying fit and active.

You need to find a place you are comfortable with that has credentials that can be verified. You'll want to be at a place where you can heal and in an environment that is peaceful and professional.

One of the first things that will happen to you when you quit drugs is detoxification. This is where all traces of the drug are removed from your body. You should not try to detox without the help of a doctor, and the rehab center will have medical staff to help you through. There are also some drugs that can aid in detox that you might be given, of course under a doctor's supervision. The next chapter gives more in-depth information about detoxification.

You will be part of a community of individuals all trying to get help for their addictions. Many rehab centers operate as a small community and decisions about life at the center are often made collaboratively.

You may be required to take classes or attend lectures about various aspects of drug addiction. These are important because they can help you lay a foundation for life after you are released from the program.

You will also probably have group therapy which will entail talking to others and listening to what they have to say. Participation in this program will help you get support from other people who are struggling with addiction. When you have other people who are going through the same things that you are, it will help you build a stable mind knowing that you have support through this venue.

Individual counseling is also part of a drug rehab program. Through individual counseling, you will be able to identify your triggers and the specific reasons why you began using and abusing drugs in the first place. You will be given ways to cope with stressors of life and techniques that you can use to help you stay away from drugs once your rehab program has finished.

Exercise and healthy eating programs will also be a big part of your recovery program. When you eat better and are active, you are better able to heal and concentrate on getting off of drugs.

The twelve-step program will most likely be introduced to you if you're not already familiar with it. This type of program has proven to be quite effective and the steps, when followed, lead to a type of inner peace that will help you stay strong against your addictions and not fall into the same rut that led you there.

Rehab facilities will teach you about meditation, yoga, eating healthy, and so much more. They can be scary and overwhelming, but they will be intense. You may find yourself angry or resistant, but when you are in a rehab facility, realize that you are there because your drug use got out of control and was damaging your life.

The people in these centers are very supportive and will do everything they can to help you through the process of becoming drug-free. Whether you are there voluntarily or have been ordered into the center for whatever reason, you need to facilitate your healing and make it as easy as possible on yourself.

Expect to eat healthier, meet new people, and talk about your problems. You may find it very liberating and when you let the program work for you instead of working against the program, you will be well on your way to a drug free lifestyle.

During your recovery process, the first step is to rid the drugs from your body. This is called detoxification and it can be very serious if you don't handle it in the correct way.

Chapter 13 - Safe Detoxing

Drug detox is the most important part of becoming free from addiction, and because of this drug detox should be handled with great care. Drug detox is a medical procedure. Drug detox should be handled in a medical facility under great supervision.

The reason for this is because drug detox can be fatal. What happens to the body when one becomes addicted is a chemical change, and to take this chemical away from the body all at once without proper care from the drug detox can turn from a positive process to a fatal one.

If you elect to enter a rehab facility, you will have the guidance and help you need to get through the detox procedure. However, if you decide outpatient rehab is more your speed, you must contact a doctor and be under his or her supervision while you are ridding your body of drugs.

The physical symptoms of detoxification vary according to what type of drugs you are coming off of. Because there are thousands of chemical reactions that occur in our body as a result of the drugs, taking the drug away will affect those chemical reactions.

Symptoms range from cold sweats to shaking to things as serious as convulsions and heart palpitations. Here is what you can expect from specific drugs:

- <u>Stimulants – Cocaine, amphetamines</u> – These drugs enhance nerve cell signaling. As a result, the nerve's native signaling chemicals are depleted. This and sleep disturbance are the neuro-biochemical reasons for the "come down" from cocaine and speed.

- <u>Benzodiazapenes – Valium, Xanax, Ativan, Ambien</u> – Drugs in this category turn down the signal of nerve cells. They make you sleepy and relaxed. When these drugs are stopped, the nerves are sensitive to the smallest stimulation. Taking these drugs out of your system will make you very jittery and shaky. You may have trouble sleeping, and in severe cases, you could have convulsions.

- <u>Alcohol</u> – Alcohol is a very subtle foe and a sneaky drug. Initially, consuming alcohol can make you energized and focused, but after a few drinks, the sedative effects kick in making you relaxed and clumsy. In your brain, millions of chemical reactions are taking place. The brain becomes more sensitivity to cope with those sedative effects. An abrupt cessation of alcohol can cause seizures or even heart attack. Hallucinations, sleep disturbance, and anxiety can occur as well.

- <u>Opiates – Heroin, Vicodin</u> – These drugs are used as pain killers and are meant to soothe and calm the body. Withdrawal from opiates can be particularly painful and severe. Expect sweating, severe muscle aches, nausea, and intense cravings. Because these symptoms are so painful, detoxing from opiates often lead addicts to begin using again.

Medical technology has provided specific drugs that can help with detoxification symptoms. I know it sounds odd – take a drug to get off a drug – but because some of the symptoms are so severe, having these drugs available can be very important. Plus, they are not addictive, and when you are under the care of a doctor, they will monitor your usage very carefully until you won't have to take those drugs anymore.

One very effective treatment of opiate withdrawal symptoms is methadone maintenance therapy. It is safe when administered under the care of a doctor. Taken orally once a day, methadone suppresses narcotic withdrawal for between 24 and 36 hours. Because methadone is effective in eliminating withdrawal symptoms, it is used in detoxifying opiate addicts. It is, however, only effective in cases of addiction to heroin, morphine, and other opioid drugs, and it is not an effective treatment for other drugs of abuse.

Methadone reduces the cravings associated with heroin use and blocks the high from heroin, but it does not provide the euphoric rush. Consequently, methadone patients do not experience the extreme highs and lows that result from the waxing and waning of heroin in blood levels. Ultimately, the patient remains physically dependent on the opioid, but is freed from the uncontrolled, compulsive, and disruptive behavior seen in heroin addicts.

Withdrawal from methadone is much slower than that from heroin. As a result, it is possible to maintain an addict on methadone without harsh side effects. Many MMT patients require continuous treatment, sometimes over a period of years.

Physicians and individualized health care give medically prescribed methadone to relieve withdrawal symptoms, reduce the opiate craving, and bring about a biochemical balance in the body. Important elements in heroin treatment include comprehensive social and rehabilitation services.

When methadone is taken under medical supervision, long-term maintenance causes no adverse effects to the heart, lungs, liver, kidneys, bones, blood, brain, or other vital body organs. Methadone produces no serious side effects, although some patients experience minor symptoms such as constipation, water retention, drowsiness, skin rash, excessive sweating, and changes in libido. Once methadone dosage is adjusted and stabilized or tolerance increases, these symptoms usually subside.

Methadone does not impair cognitive functions. It has no adverse effects on mental capability, intelligence, or employability. It is not sedating or intoxicating, nor does it interfere with ordinary activities such as driving a car or operating machinery. Patients are able to feel pain and experience emotional reactions. Most importantly, methadone relieves the craving associated with opiate addiction. For methadone patients, typical street doses of heroin are ineffective at producing euphoria, making the use of heroin less desirable.

Another huge part of safe detoxification has to do with nutrition. Because the body will be going through some harsh abuse, it's important that your body is at its strongest. That means eating healthy and getting some form of exercise. You may want to consult with a nutritionist to be sure that you are getting the proper nutrition, but you CAN simply make your own changes in what you eat so your body is at its peak level of performance.

You will also want to get some psychological help with a counselor or therapist. You must treat your mental state along with your body. The therapist can help you remain focused on your recovery and take away some of the mindsets that can hinder your recovery.

As we said previously, twelve step programs have proven to be very effective in overcoming problems with addiction. These can be great self-help options.

Chapter 14 - Working The 12 Steps

The original 12 step formula was developed by Alcoholics Anonymous as a way for people to deal with their powerlessness over alcohol. Since then, other 12 step programs have evolved for a variety of addictions including Narcotics Anonymous, Gambler's Anonymous, and Al-Anon.

All 12 step programs follow similar patterns. Members meet regularly to discuss their experiences, strength, and hope. One common view is that all members are dealing with an illness and an addiction rather than a bad habit or poor lifestyle. The idea is that recovery will occur by taking individual responsibility for one's own recovery and relying on the will of a Higher Power while following the 12 steps.

One of the most widely recognized portions of a 12 step group is the requirement that members admit that they have a problem. That's why many members open their addresses to the group with their name and the admission of their problem.

Attendees at group meetings share their experiences, challenges, successes, and failures. They also provide peer support for each other. Many people who have joined these groups say they found success that they were unable to find before.

The 12 steps as outlined by Alcoholics Anonymous are:

1) We admitted we were powerless over alcohol and that our lives had become unmanageable.

2) We have come to believe that a power greater than ourselves could restore us to sanity.

3) We have made a decision to turn our will and our lives over to the care of God as we understand him.

4) We make a searching a fearless moral inventory of our lives and ourselves.

5) We admit to God, to ourselves, and to another human being the exact nature of our wrongs.

6) We are entirely ready to have God remove all these defects of character.

7) We humbly ask Him to remove our shortcoming.

8) We make a list of all persons we have harmed and are willing to make amends to all of them.

9) We make direct amends to such people wherever possible, except when to do so would injure them or others.

10) We continue to take personal inventory and when we are wrong, we promptly admit it.

11) Through prayer and meditation, we seek to improve our conscious contact with God, as we understand Him, praying only for knowledge of His will for us and the power to carry that out.

12) Having had a spiritual awakening as the result of these steps, we carry this message to other addicts and practice these principles in all our affairs.

Members of a 12 step program also make several promises to themselves and to others. These promises are:

- If we are painstaking about this phase of our development, we will be amazed before we are halfway through.

- We are going to know a new freedom and a new happiness.

- We will not regret the past nor wish to shut the door on it.

- We will comprehend the word "serenity" and we will know peace.

- No matter how far down the scale we have gone, we will see how our experiences can benefit others.

- The feeling of uselessness and self-pity will disappear.

- We will lose interest in selfish things and gain interest in our fellow man.

- Self-seeking will slip away.

- Our whole attitude and outlook on life will change.

- Fear of people and economic insecurity will leave us.

- We will intuitively know how to handle situations that used to challenge us.

- We will suddenly realize that God is doing for us what we could not do for ourselves.

Opponents of 12 step programs are put off by the use of the words "Higher Power" and God in their steps and mottos. They say that this is pushing religion on people and is morally wrong if that person doesn't believe in God in the same way as others do.

However, you should know that AA and other similar groups are not religious groups. That is why the verbage "Higher Power" is used along with the phrase "God, as we understand Him to be". The purpose of 12 step programs is to simply deliver addicts from their destructive behaviors and help them become clean and sober. It is a spiritual program in nature, not a religious program.

Many people are apprehensive about appearing in front of strangers and sharing their most personal information. Please remember that 12 step programs are anonymous. Only your first name is shared.

If you live in a small town, you may worry that people will recognize you, but keep in mind that those other people are there for the same reason you are and they want to remain anonymous just like you. You may be surprised at the camaraderie you will find when you are with people who share the same experiences that you do.

One of the possible reasons you became addicted to drugs is due to low self-esteem. You need to address self-esteem issues early on in your recovery.

Chapter 15 - Building Your Self-Esteem

It is nearly impossible to effectively journey down the path to recovery without realizing that you deserve to be drug-free. Building your self-esteem requires effort on your part, and, just like during your self-assessment, it also requires personal honesty. Building self esteem helps not only with personal acceptance, but with staying strong during your recovery as well.

To begin with, you need to answer a few questions:

- Do I deserve happiness in my life?

- Should I expect to be accepted by others?

- What do I want out of life?

When you answer these questions honestly, you can begin to acknowledge your strengths and weaknesses. Accepting that you have certain strengths and weaknesses can help you concentrate on the parts of you that need to be worked on and what can help you through.

Remember, you are a unique individual and are no less worthy than anyone else in what you deserve from life. If you hesitated to answer, or answered negatively to any of the questions above, please keep reading. You create your own tomorrow today. Changing a thought process or your inner expectations is essential to recovery.

Positive affirmations are very important in building your self esteem. They will become your mantra as you work on the parts of you that you want to change. They can also be helpful when you are feeling weak during the recovery process.

A positive affirmation can be anything you want it to be, but it must be positive! Here are a few to consider:

- I deserve to be happy.

- I am a person worthy of respect and acceptance from those around me.

- It's OK to accept a compliment

- I believe that my life has meaning.

- I am a wonderful person who deserves to be sober.

- When I become more confident, I can do anything.

- I am strong and can make it through today.

- I am more than a body, I am a soul and a heart and a spirit and those are parts of me that have to heal so I can be healthy.

Look in the mirror, look into your own eyes, and recite your affirmation over and over again. Change your mindset from not believing what you say to wholeheartedly accepting that it is the truth. Do this several times a day if you have to. Eventually, you'll start believing what you say without having to quiet down those negative thoughts when they creep in.

A part of having low self esteem involves self pity. Feeling sorry for yourself when things get rough is a common factor among people with low self esteem and especially among addicts. Many people listen to their negative inner voices because it's become a way of life. Self pity robs you of the joys of life and makes you helpless against your inner demons.

When bad things happen to you, try to focus on the positive things that can come of it. Make time for yourself to recite your positive affirmations. Work hard on focusing on the positives of life. When you're overwhelmed, think, "I'm still alive and I need to be thankful for that."

You may want to try mind mapping. This is a technique used by teachers all over the world and it can do wonders for you when keeping in mind your ultimate goals.

Take a piece of paper and make a circle in the center. Inside that circle, write one of your goals. Then take a line and draw it out from the circle. On that line, write a way you can go about achieving that goal. You may want to list things to avoid by starting with "Don't" or "Not". Make as many "feelers" as you need to.

Once you have your mind map done, carry it with you or post it someplace where you will see it every day. When you have the map to refer to, you will be focusing on your goals and getting away from what will hold you back from seeing those goals realized.

Another step towards building self esteem is to realize that you, as a person, have certain rights. These rights extend to more than just those guaranteed in the constitution. We're talking about moral and ethical rights that you are entitled to. These include the right to:

- Make your own decisions
- Pleasing yourself before you try to please others
- Dignity and respect
- Say "No" if you don't want to do something
- Live without abuse and control from others
- Make mistakes and then learn from them
- Be treated like you treat others, which should be respectfully

The foundation for building self esteem to engage in codependency and addiction recovery, is built by returning to the child of innocence within. Study and do your own work to become whole, remember this is for your healing. Each person is different and becoming whole will depend on what an individual's experiences have been. The only person in your life at all times and the only one who knows the truth from your perspective is you. Stand for the truth in you.

Having the support of your family is also crucial during your recovery period. If you are a family member who has a loved one with an addiction, this is an especially important chapter for you.

Chapter 16 - Involving The Family

Your family probably already knows you have a drug addiction. If they don't, admitting your dependence to them is a crucial step towards recovery. Sit them down and be as honest with them as you have been with yourself. It probably won't be fun and it most likely won't be pretty, but as soon as you have that off of your chest, you'll be free to start pursuing your goal of being drug-free.

Tell your family members that you want their support in your endeavor and that it's important for you to know that you can count on them to give that support. If they don't, just accept it and move on yourself. Some people just can't be that strong, but if you are sincere in your request, they will most likely be as supportive as you need them to be.

Your family needs to be supportive without becoming enablers. Remind them that you need them to be supportive of your decision and be available if you need to talk. But also tell them that it is not their responsibility to cover up your mistakes, relapses, or problems.

At all times, you need to respect them and show them that you appreciate their support. As difficult as it might be for you, it's doubly as difficult for them to watch you going through the pain that you are.

As a family member, here are some things you can do to support your addict.

- Remind them to attend any meetings they need to (AA, NA, etc.)

- Do not loan them money

- Participate in group therapy if asked

- Encourage them to eat healthy and exercise

- Point out when they are engaging in damaging behavior

- Be open to listen when he or she wants to talk

- Don't try to solve all their problems

You may have to change the way you celebrate family events. This is especially true with people who are trying to overcome alcohol addiction. Often, when some families get together, alcohol is a big part of the celebration. Be understanding if your family member with a problem doesn't want to attend a function.

Try to keep alcohol in a separate place where they can't get to it. DO NOT, under any circumstances poke fun at them or try to get them to join in. They are having a hard enough time as it is – they don't need "peer" pressure on top of it all.

Generally, most families play certain roles during the addiction and recovery process. See if you or your family fits into any of these roles:

- The Addict: The person with the addiction is at the center. They are not necessarily most important, however, they will be the center of attention. After all, their addiction is the issue at hand. The rest of you will assume other roles around the addict.

- The Hero: This is the person who feels they have to make all family members "look good" in the eyes of others. They often ignore the problem and present things in a positive light as if the problem didn't exist. The Hero is the perfectionist demanding more of The Addict than he or she can provide.

- <u>The Mascot</u>: The Mascot will often try to inject humor into the situation. Sometimes this humor is inappropriate and can hinder the recovery process. The Mascot is also the cheerleader providing support where possible.

- <u>The Lost Child</u>: This is the silent person who always seems to be in the way or left out. They are quiet and reserved not making problems. The Lost Child gives up self needs and tries to avoid conversation regarding the problem.

- <u>The Scapegoat</u>: This person often acts out in front of others. They divert attention from The Addict and the problems that you are all facing together.

- <u>The Caretaker</u>: This person is the enabler. They try to keep the whole family happy and keep all roles in balance. They often make excuses for The Addict's behavior and puts on a happy front for outsiders. The Caretaker denies that there's any problem and usually never mention anything about addiction or recovery.

The parts played by family members lead to codependency. Members make decisions concerning what the other person needs. Codependency leads to aversion and lack of self orientation in a situation where an addiction is present. Ultimately people "become" the part they are playing.

The goal in alcohol and drug addiction recovery is to bring each member as a whole into a situation where the problems can be dealt with. Individual talents and abilities should be integrated into the situation, allowing emotional honesty about the situation, without guilt or punishment.

People become familiar with and dependent on the role they play in families. In overcoming the family roles, you will begin to overcome issues, and what could be classified as the addiction to the role. While conquering the substance is important to the person with the addiction, a point to remember is the substance(s) is not the key to family recovery, removing the underlying roles are.

In beginning recovery, each family member must become proactive against the addiction to the role, and learn to become their true self. The goal is for each to person to become independent, and then approach the substance addiction recovery as a group of individuals, rather than as people playing a part. Whole, independent people can freely contribute to the recovery of the person overcoming the addiction, while a person playing a part can only perform the role.

Each family member must realize which role they play and then start thinking about how to change that role or make it work to the advantage of The Addict. Working together is a must when it comes to getting a loved one off of drugs. Make a list of strengths and weaknesses then assess that list to see how you can use your strengths to help The Addict without bringing your weaknesses into play.

Realize that the process and that role contributes in some way toward helping. Family members should acknowledge their individual parts in this process and acknowledge that they have an integral role that in unique to them. Each person is just as important as the other.

As a family, you have to prepare to be flexible. Overcoming drug addiction is a difficult journey – one that is met with bumps and dips and curves. Life can change from day to day even hour to hour. You need to "roll with the punches" and adapt to whatever situation is thrown at you in the whole process.

As a family member, you may want to consider having an intervention. How do you do that?

Chapter 17 - Interventions

Anytime someone needs help but refuses to accept it, a family intervention is appropriate. A family intervention can be used for people engaged in any self-destructive behavior and especially appropriate for addicts.

Intervention is the most loving, powerful and successful method yet for helping people accept help. A family intervention can be done with love and respect in a non-confrontational, non-judgmental manner. A family intervention is often the answer, the only answer. It can be done. It can be done now.

It certainly is not an easy decision to make when you are considering intervention for a loved one's problems. But if you are able to handle it in a loving, caring manner, you will be giving that loved one a gift that they will appreciate – eventually!

The first thing that needs to be done is that all family members and friends who might be able to make a difference must agree on a time and place to meet. It's a good idea to contact a professional counselor to help you.

You may initially be apprehensive and confused. Members participating in the intervention may be ambivalent about whether or not to actually do the intervention. Some may be afraid of the person, others may be angry. The goal is to move from this disorganized and chaotic state to a cohesive, focused group.

To do this, the participants meet with the leader beforehand to educate themselves about the dysfunction, to determine how to best help themselves, and to prepare for Intervention Day. This includes identifying others who should be involved , exploring appropriate treatment options, and preparing what they are going to say.

This preparation often involves several meetings, telephone calls, and culminates in a practice session immediately prior to the Intervention Day. The time varies, but the process is usually contained within one to two weeks. Sometimes it can be shortened to a weekend.

It is important for all of you to meet prior to Intervention Day so that you can discuss what steps will be taken and how you will be approaching the person you are trying to help. Remember that you need to work together as a unit and decide what will be said beforehand.

You then need to get the person you want to help to actually show up. This can be accomplished in many ways. Use your imagination and say what you have to in order for the addicted person to arrive at the designated place.

There is no absolute right way to intervene in someone else's life. In fact, there is a school of thought that argues that any form of intervention is abhorrent, a violation of free speech and of an individual's right to choose. Nevertheless, as individuals and as a society we are always influencing others whether or not we want to, and sometimes we decide to intervene purposefully.

Intervention can be simple or it can be more involved. The decision about what type of intervention to conduct must be up to all participating parties.

A simple intervention is exactly what it sounds like. You simply ask the person you are intervening for to get help for their problem. Believe it or not, sometimes this works incredibly well. Often an addict is just waiting for someone else to acknowledge their problem before they do. Once they know that everyone can see the problem, they are given permission to seek help with the support of their family and friends.

If a situation has reached dangerous proportions where a person's life is in danger, a crisis intervention is necessary. Crisis Interventions occur in dangerous situations involving reckless driving, weapons, hospital emergency rooms, or violence or threats of violence. It is obvious in these situations that a person is in immediate danger to himself or others.

The immediate objective in these cases is to calm the crisis and to create safety for all. Remember, a crisis often creates golden opportunities for family members to help someone accept help.

A classical intervention requires all attention to be focused on the addict. Participants are often asked to talk with the addict and tell them what their addiction has done to them personally. It's very important to be brutally honest during these discussions. Let it all go – this is the perfect opportunity.

Expect the addict to be defensive. That's normal. They will probably deny that they even have a problem at all. They'll most likely yell and scream or try to get away. The purpose of an intervention is to get everyone's feelings out into the open, so the person you are trying to help should not be allowed to leave the room. However, avoid violence.

Your ultimate goal with an intervention is to persuade your loved one to get help with his or her addiction. If it's bad enough to warrant an intervention, you will probably want to suggest an in-patient rehabilitation center. At the very least, you should have the names and numbers of several different services they can turn to for help.

Be sure that your tone is sympathetic but helpful and that the person you are trying to help knows without a doubt that they have your support. Intervention can be an effective tool in the process of recovery, but it must be handled in the right way which is why we strongly suggest the help of a professional.

There are certain things that can severely hinder the recovery process.

Chapter 18 - Staying Sober

You did not become a drug addict overnight. It was a long process occurring over a period of, perhaps, several years that turned into a dependence on those drugs. You began using probably primarily because you needed an escape. It's very important that you remove anything in your life that could cause you to begin using again.

This begins with changing your life and the people around you. Your friends probably played a big role in getting you to start using in the first place. Peer pressure is difficult to overcome and when you are around people using drugs, your recovery is seriously compromised.

Many people hate this part of drug recovery. But you have to keep in mind what is best for you. True friends will stay with you and maybe even help you. Those who got you to use in the first place will be the ones who will stay away from you. Their drug use will be much more important to them than you are. Remember this.

During initial recovery stages, you will want to avoid situations where you might be tempted to use. For example, if you are trying to stop drinking, keep away from social situations and locations that may make it more difficult for you to not drink. That means no bars or clubs and not going to parties where alcohol is served. Think about the places where you used drugs and avoid them at all costs.

Eventually, you will become stronger and more able to resist the temptation especially after a period of time has passed.

We can't stress enough the advantages of counseling during drug withdrawal. The biggest mistake you can make is to not seek help. You have a very powerful force working in you wanting you to use again. Therapy can help you stay strong against these inner demons and teach you new ways to deal with stress and anxiety that could have pushed you towards drugs in the first place.

Even if you are not a religious person, it's a good idea to acknowledge that there is a higher power affecting our lives. We are here for a reason and came to be what we are because of certain factors that we just can't explain.

For example, there is a set of unwritten "rules" that we just know for no explainable reason. Those rules came from a higher power. Whether you call him (or her) God, Buddha, or whatever, that power exists somewhere.

This book isn't meant to be a religious dissertation, so we'll let you make whatever decision you need to regarding this higher power, but please know that your recovery will be much easier when you have this power in your life.

You may want to explore some other avenues for peace in your mind and body.

Chapter 19 - Calming The Soul

Meditation can be a very effective way to overcome the powerful reactions that occur in your mind during drug withdrawal. Your inner voices will be telling you all sorts of different things when you are trying to get off drugs. If you recognize these damaging inner voices and take steps to calm them, your chance to successfully recover is significantly increased.

If you take a moment and practice some meditation techniques, your body will calm and those voices will go away. We could make an entire book on meditation – in fact, we have! However, following are some basic meditation exercises you can try.

First, you need to be in a quiet place free of distractions. Get comfortable and allow yourself a little bit of time to relax and be open to the meditations. You will be focusing your mind on an object of thought or awareness and acknowledging where your mindset is now and where you want it to be.

The first stage in meditation is to stop distractions and make your mind more lucid and clearer. This can be accomplished through simple breathing meditation. Sit in a position that is comfortable for you. You may want to try sitting cross legged keeping your spine straight and resting your arms comfortably in your lap.

Close your eyes and focus on your breathing. Breathe naturally through your nose. Don't try to control your breathing, simply become aware of the air coming in and out of your nose. Feel the sensation of the breath with each inhalation and exhalation.

At first, your mind will be very busy and you might think the meditation isn't working. But what you are doing is becoming aware of just how busy your mind is. Resist following thoughts as they arise. Just concentrate on your breaths and how they feel. If you find your mind wandering, just bring it back to the breathing. Keep doing this as many times as is necessary.

Meditation requires great patience. You can't control your thoughts unless you train yourself to do so. Practice breathing meditation as often as you can. With time and practice, you will find yourself slipping into the state of mind you need to be in much quicker.

When you exhale, you may want to try humming or repeating a word over and over. We like to use the word "Peace" or "Serenity", but you can choose whatever word will calm you.

Buddhist meditation suggests that you say your chosen phrase or word during inhalation. Their phrase is generally "Ham Sah" which means "I am that." Then when you exhale, say "Saah" which should sound like a sigh. They find this very relaxing and it helps them get in touch with their inner thoughts.

In researching this book, we found a great website you may want to visit. At www.learningmeditation.com, you can go to their meditation room where they have various recorded meditations you can listen to that will help you relax and feel renewed. When you concentrate on the voice that is speaking, you can become more focused and relax.

Another good technique is to picture a relaxing place for you. This might be a sunny beach or in a warm bath. Wherever you are most relaxed is where you should picture in your head. Imagine you are there and feel the sensations that the image conjures up.

You can also use progressive muscle relaxation to get rid of your stress. PMR involves concentrating on one part of the body at a time. Start with your right leg. Tighten the muscles in your leg and hold the tightening for a few seconds – a count of ten perhaps. Then relax those muscles feeling the sensation that you get with that relaxation. Move on to each part of your body using the same technique until you have covered them all.

Exercise is great for stress relief. You may want to look into yoga classes. Yoga is a very spiritual exercise method and can do wonders for stress relief. Tai Chi is another spiritual form of exercise that requires you to concentrate on your body rather than your mind. When you do that, you will find yourself becoming much more relaxed and able to cope with the world.

There is one aspect of drug addiction that we haven't addressed yet, and we would be remiss if we didn't acknowledge this growing problem.

Chapter 20 - Teens And Drugs

The statistics are alarming. Teen drug abuse is and has been on the rise for many years. Consider the following numbers calculated in 2005:

- 8th grade -- 30.3%

- 10th grade -- 44.9%

- 12th grade -- 52.8%

Those numbers measure the percentage of teenagers who regularly use illegal drugs of some type. Just within the last month, 50 percent of teens report drinking alcohol with 37 percent saying they had been drunk on at least one occasion. Alcohol kills 5 times more teenagers than any other drug – mostly from accidents.

It's scary to think that our young people are being exposed to drugs at a much earlier age, and they are much more susceptible to peer pressure. When their friends offer up drugs, they often don't have the strength to say no, so they begin the frightening cycle of drug abuse.

In recent years, much has been learned about the health effects of teen drug use. Drugs are readily available to those who choose to use them in either an "experimental" way or to those who are chronic drug abusers. The consequence of such use, even causal use, can be devastating to both the user and to the user's family members.

But, teen drug use is costly to more than just families. It is especially costly to our society as a whole. Youth's immature physical, emotional, and psychological development make them MORE susceptible than adults to the harmful effects of drug abuse.

In the 7 years that the National Center on Addiction and Substance Abuse (CASA) at Columbia University has published the National Survey of American Attitudes on Substance Abuse, results have indicated that teens and their parents view drugs as their biggest concern.

The health effects of teen drug use can vary, depending on such factors as frequency of use, the kind of drug taken, how much is taken, how quickly it gets into the brain, what other drugs are taken at the same time, the differences in body size and chemistry, the length of time the drugs are used, and other components.

Why do teens use drugs? Of course, peer pressure is a huge factor, but they succumb to peer pressure for many other reasons. Low self-esteem, depression, anxiety, inability to express feelings, lack of control, and feeling like they have to live up to unrealistic parental expectations all contribute to the teen beginning to use drugs. Plus, many teens are affected by watching their parents' own addictive behaviors

Trying to deal with issues revolving around the family upon such an escalated level proves extremely difficult when children of alcoholic parents cannot even function normally regarding their own lives. This situation often spawns a codependency syndrome that follows the child throughout his or her entire life; codependency has long been found to be a significant indicator of alcoholism

And, believe it or not, parents who overindulge their children may be dealing with a teenager drug user before they know it. Many parents spoil their children not only with toys and gadgets but also by not setting limits for them. That freedom leads them to make bad decisions about their lives which includes drug and alcohol use.

So how do you know if your teen is using drugs? There are some warning signs you should be looking for. When at home, see if any of these warning signs appear:

- loss of interest in family activities

- disrespect for family rules

- withdrawal from responsibilities

- verbally or physically abusive

- sudden increase or decrease in appetite

- disappearance of valuable items or money

- not coming home on time

- not telling you where they are going

- constant excuses for behavior

- spending a lot of time in their rooms

- lies about activities

- finding the following: cigarette rolling papers, pipes, roach clips, small glass vials, plastic baggies, remnants of drugs (seeds, etc.)
- When it comes to school, there are also some indicators to watch for:
- sudden drop in grades
- truancy
- loss of interest in learning
- sleeping in class
- poor work performance
- not doing homework
- defiant of authority
- poor attitude towards sports or other extracurricular activities
- reduced memory and attention span
- not informing you of teacher meetings, open houses, etc.
- Physically and emotionally, they may have one of the following behaviors:
- changes friends
- smell of alcohol or marijuana on breath or body

- unexplainable mood swings and behavior
- negative, argumentative, paranoid or confused, destructive, anxious
- over-reacts to criticism acts rebellious
- sharing few if any of their personal problems
- doesn't seem as happy as they used to be
- overly tired or hyperactive
- drastic weight loss or gain
- unhappy and depressed
- cheats, steals
- always needs money, or has excessive amounts of money
- sloppiness in appearance

If your teen exhibits six or more of these signs over a period of a few weeks, he or she probably is using drugs. You need to address it as soon as you suspect this to be true.

The most effective tool against teen drug use is communication. When you pair open communication with education, you have double the ammunition to fight drug use.

Your first inclination might be to get angry when you find out your teen is using drugs. This a normal reaction, but please know that anger and yelling will just turn your teen's ears to the "off" position. You need to let your teen know you care about them and that you just want the best for them.

You must place responsibility for their actions on their own shoulders and make them accountable without doing so in a threatening manner. Honest, open communication is the key towards overcoming your teen's problem – even before it becomes a problem.

Move on to the future and find things that you can do right now to help your teen. Try not to live in past; this will make the person you are trying to help agitated or upset. With addiction comes a lot of damage; material and emotional. In the wake of the episodes that the addict can create, remember that you are not alone. There are people around you that care. Those that have been and are in the trenches of this disease can help the addict when no one else can.

Counseling is a very effective way to help curb your teen's drug use. By allowing your child to interact with a third party you will find that recovery often goes better, because often times the family is too emotionally close to the addict to be of any real help.

Please realize that you are the parents and you are not responsible for the disease of addiction. Get help before it is too late. Remember that this disease does not discriminate against anyone or anything.

No single treatment is appropriate for all teens which is why there are many places your teen can get help. Look for local programs geared towards teens and find a peer counselor who your teen can talk to. Teens relate to other teens and young people, so finding someone close to their own age can be very effective.

Match the treatment with the individual. If your teen's drug use has gotten completely out of hand, you may want to look at an inpatient clinic. But try to find a clinic where other teens are being treated as well. If you send them to a program that has only adults in it, their chances of relapse are higher.

If you do put your teen in a treatment facility, be sure you participate in all of the activities that are asked of you. This is the perfect time for your teen to talk to you in a safe environment with a moderator. They are more likely to open up and say what they need to say in the clinic rather than at home.

Just as with adults, relapse is a very real possibility, neigh, a probability. Teens are going to be thrust back into the environment that they were in when they were users, so keep in mind that drug addiction is a very powerful mental disease and relapses are very likely to occur.

This is where patience and understanding come in. Talk with your teen and get them help and counseling to understand why they went back to drugs. When you tackle the psychological part of drug abuse, you have a better chance of helping your teen become drug free.

It's also important for you to educate your child BEFORE drug use becomes a problem. Again, we say, communicate openly and honestly with your child and arm them with as much information as you can possibly find. There has been a push to get drug information in the schools, but don't leave it all up to them.

You are your child's best defense against drugs. While they may be uncomfortable when you present them with information, they'll thank you later in life. It's kind of like having "the sex talk" – it's awkward for both of you, but it's something that is necessary.

Teach them how to say no without feeling guilty. Show them that they are a valued and loved person and that they have the right to refuse something that is not good for them. Tell them the types of people to avoid and the things they can say if they are offered drugs or find themselves in a compromising situation.

As a parent, you will need your own support to deal with this difficult situation. There are two great organizations that are there to help parents of drug addicted teens. They are:

www.becauseiloveyou.org

and

www.familiesanonymous.org

Both of these organizations have a multitude of information on their websites. They provide you with tools to help attack the problem and deal with your own mental health as well as that of your child.

Families Anonymous is also very helpful with anyone who has a loved one who is addicted to drugs.

Support groups can be very powerful in helping you remain strong for your child. They can then draw off that strength and remain drug-free. You are your child's best weapon against the things out there in the world that want to harm them. Don't let them down.

Conclusion

Drug addiction is a powerful demon that can sneak up on you and take over your life before you know it has even happened. What started out as just a recreational lifestyle has overcome your life and affected every single aspect of it.

You don't have to be caught up in the web of drug addiction. There are so many things you can do to get yourself clean and sober, and there's no better time than the present.

This book isn't meant to be a specific treatment plan. It is just a guide to help get you on the road to sobriety. We are not medical professionals. We have just brought together information and advice from some of the professional and medical organizations out there to guide you on your recovery journey.

Overcoming drug addiction is a long and often painful process. There is much that you need to know before you start and that's why we wanted to give you this book.

Leading a clean lifestyle is something that is well within your reach. You now have the tools you need – go out and heal yourself. Remember that a thousand mile journey always begins with one step and to take it one day at a time. You can do it!